Women
Inventors
by Sandra Ortiz

HOUGHTON MIFFLIN   BOSTON

TABLE OF CONTENTS

INTRODUCTION

Inventors are people who come up with ideas for machines and other items. If the idea for the invention is original, meaning it's never been done before, the government gives a patent. A patent states that the inventor owns the idea. He or she can make the item and make money from its sales.

Can you imagine a car without windshield wipers? Do you think dishwashers and cordless phones make things easier? Women inventors created these machines and others that help our lives.

A woman invented the cordless phone, an invention you may use every day.

Sybilla Masters

In 1715, American colonist Sybilla Masters invented a machine to clean and grind corn so that it could be used for cloth and food. The device used hammers to grind down the maize, the corn from the Native Americans.

England's King George I gave Masters much praise or her invention. Even with this public credit, the British courts would not award a patent to Masters because she was a woman. Instead, they awarded the patent — the first American patent – to Masters husband, Thomas Masters!

CATHARINE GREENE

One of the most important American inventions was the cotton gin, patented in 1794.

As the story goes, Eli Whitney was a tutor for Catharine Littlefield Greene's children. Eli and Catharine were both interested in machines. One day, Catharine challenged Eli to create a machine to pull cotton from the plant so the cotton could be used for clothing. Some say that she gave Eli the drawings for the machine.

It's thought that the cotton gin was Catharine's idea, and she paid to have it made. In any case, Eli Whitney received the patent and the credit for the invention.

Eli Whitney is given credit for inventing the cotton gin, but Catharine Greene helped him.

MARGARET KNIGHT

Margaret Knight, known as Mattie, was inventive at a very young age. When she was 12 years old, Mattie visited her brother at the New England textile mill where he worked. A worker was injured by a machine. Right then, Mattie came up with the idea for machines to include stop buttons so workers could turn off machines in emergencies.

Margaret Knight invented this machine for folding and pasting paper bags.

Margaret Knight's invention helped workers make paper bags with a flat, square bottom.

As an adult, Mattie went to work in a paper bag factory. Factory workers spent a lot of time making paper bags by hand. Mattie worked hard to create a machine that would help them make a paper bag. The machine was patented in 1870. A similar machine is still used today.

Margaret Knight had many patented inventions. She earned the nickname the "woman Edison," after the famous inventor Thomas Edison.

The U.S. Navy won many battles because of Martha Coston's invention.

MARTHA COSTON

Some inventors take a great idea and make it better. Martha Coston's husband was a scientist for the U.S. Navy. After he died, Martha read a diary that he had kept. There she found an idea that he had. His idea was that the Navy could use flares in the night sky to signal to the shore and other ships at sea.

Martha took the idea and improved it. She received a patent in 1871. The night signals were made from pyrotechnics, or fireworks. Each fireworks container was twisted to ignite. Different colors and patterns told different messages.

The clothes wringer became very popular.

Ellen Eglin

Inventive women weren't always given credit for their ideas. Sometime in the 1880s, an African American woman named Ellen Eglin invented a machine to wring water from washed clothes. Before her invention, water from every washed shirt, pair of pants, or socks or to be squeezed out by hand. This took a lot of time and strength.

Ellen sold her idea for $18. The person who bought Ellen's idea made a lot of money.

Hotels and restaurants were the first to buy Josephine's dishwasher.

JOSEPHINE COCHRAN

Josephine Cochran's model of the automatic dishwasher wasn't the first automatic dishwasher that was invented. However, her model, patented in 1886, was the first one that really worked!

The secret was water pressure. With strong water pressure, the water and suds could get dirty dishes, pots, and pans clean.

Josephine's model was too large and too expensive for families to buy and use. It took until the 1950s — long after Josephine died in 1913 for dishwashers to become common appliances in many homes.

MARY ANDERSON

In the early 1900s, Mary Anderson was in New York City. She was riding in an electric-powered streetcar. It was snowing. Mary noticed how hard it was for the streetcar driver to see the road.

Early drivers used their hands to clear their windshields.

That snowy-day journey is how Mary came up with the idea of the windshield wiper. A T-shaped rubber blade was attached to the windshield. The driver would crank a handle inside the car to make the wiper swing back and forth. Now wipers move with the turn of a button.

HEDY LAMARR

Hedy Lamarr was a famous movie actress in the 1940s. She was also famous for being an inventor. With the help of musical composer George Antheil, Hedy created the first radio-controlled torpedo.

Before Hedy's invention, radio signals would guide the torpedo. The problem was that the enemy could pick up on the signals and change the course of the torpedo. To prevent that, Hedy's method was to change the radio frequencies quickly and without a pattern. It was a little like changing radio stations in a secret code! A torpedo device recognized the signals, but the enemy couldn't pick them up. The idea worked. The invention was patented in 1942.

Hedy Lamarr's invention helped the United States in World War II.

TERI PALL

While Alexander Graham Bell invented the telephone, one woman made it what it is today. In 1965, Teri Pall created the first cordless phone. At first she couldn't sell the idea because the sound waves got in the way of airplane signals overhead. Teri improved the model so people could use them in their homes.

For the first time, people could be mobile while talking on the phone. Teri's cordless phone was also important because it paved the way for the invention of cellular phones.

Cordless phones allow people to walk anywhere in their home and even out-of-doors.

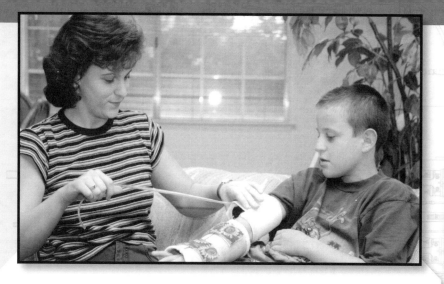

Krysta Morlan's invention helps to make the skin inside a cast more comfortable.

KRYSTA MORLAN

In 1998, California high school student Krysta Morlan had an idea for an invention. It was inspired by a need of her own. Krysta has cerebral palsy, a disease that affects the brain and muscles. She had surgery to help her walk. Krysta had to wear a cast from her hip to her ankle. It was hot, and her leg would get itchy.

Krysta created the cast cooler. A plastic tube ran cool air into a cast, thanks to a battery-charged aquarium pump. Krysta won a special award for this invention.

WOMEN'S INVENTION TABLE

1715	Indian corn mill by Sybilla Masters
1793	Cotton gin by Catharine Greene
1870	Paper-bag folding device by Margaret Knight
1871	Maritime night signals by Martha Coston
1880s	Clothes wringer by Ellen Eglin
1886	Dishwasher by Josephine Cochran
1903	Windshield wiper by Mary Anderson
1942	Secret communication system by Hedy Lamarr
1968	Cordless telephone by Teri Pall
1998	Cast cooler by Krysta Morlan